Abandoned Amusement Parks

by Dinah Williams

Consultant: Paul F. Johnston, PhD
Washington, D.C.

BEARPORT
PUBLISHING

New York, New York

Credits

Cover and Title Page, © Estelle/Shutterstock, © Lisa F. Young/Shutterstock, and © Arvind Balaraman/Shutterstock; 4–5, Kim Jones; 6, © From the collections of the Omaha Public Library; 7, Courtesy of Douglas County (NE) Historical Society Archives; 8T, Courtesy of Jeffrey Stanton; 8B, Courtesy of Jeffrey Stanton; 9, © Los Angeles Public Library Photo Collection; 10, © 2011 Elyse Pasquale; 11, © Efrem Lukatsky/Associated Press; 12, © Robert A. Hogue; 13T, © Hemera Collection/Thinkstock; 13B, © Photograph by Karen Stuebing; 14L, Courtesy of Dave Althoff, Jr.; 14R, Courtesy of Boone County Sheriff's Department; 15L, © Photo by John McDonald/LostIndiana.net; 15R, Courtesy of Dave Althoff, Jr.; 16, © Missouri Valley Special Collections, Kansas City Public Library, Kansas City, Missouri; 17, © Kansas City Public Library; 18, © Bob McMillan/FEMA Photo; 19, © Erich Valo; 20, © Niagara Falls (Ontario) Public Library; 21T, © F. H. Leslie Limited; 22, © Kelly-Mooney Photography/Corbis; 23, © Kelly-Mooney Photography/Corbis; 24, © Spinner Publications; 25, © Robert Magina; 26, © 2006 Martin Mandias Lyle; 27, © 2006 Martin Mandias Lyle; 31, © iStockphoto/Thinkstock; 32, © iStockphoto/Thinkstock.

Publisher: Kenn Goin
Editorial Director: Adam Siegel
Creative Director: Spencer Brinker
Design: Dawn Beard Creative
Cover: Kim Jones
Photo Researcher: We Research Pictures, LLC

Library of Congress Cataloging-in-Publication Data

Williams, Dinah.
  Abandoned amusement parks / by Dinah Williams.
     pages cm. — (Scary places)
  Includes bibliographical references and index.
  ISBN-13: 978-1-61772-884-6 (library binding) — ISBN-10: 1-61772-884-5 (library binding)
  1. Amusement parks—United States—History—Juvenile literature. 2. Haunted places—United States—History—Juvenile literature. I. Title.
  GV1853.2.W53 2014
  791.06'873—dc23
                                    2013011962

For more information, write to Bearport Publishing Company, Inc., 45 West 21st Street, Suite 3B, New York, New York 10010. Printed in the United States of America.

10 9 8 7 6 5 4 3 2 1

Contents

There is something both sad and creepy about an **abandoned** amusement park. Perhaps it's because a place that was once packed with fun seekers has become slowly choked with weeds. Or maybe it's because the sound of children's excited laughter has been replaced with the quiet creaking of rusted rides. When the only visitors are the spirits of those who died there many years ago, an amusement park can be a very scary place to visit.

In this book, you will visit 11 abandoned amusement parks. Within them, you will discover a roller coaster left to rot after nearly killing its passengers, deserted rides that are now home to alligators and snakes, and the ghost of a man who is trying to ride a Ferris wheel that stopped working years ago.

The Crash of the Coaster

Krug Park, Omaha, Nebraska

Krug Park introduced a number of new attractions in 1913. They included an airplane ride, a **penny arcade**, and a huge merry-go-round that had 72 horses. The most exciting attraction of all, however, was the Big Dipper roller coaster.

Krug Park

By 1930, the Big Dipper roller coaster in Krug Park had made riders scream for 17 years. That summer, however, the joyful shrieks turned to cries of pain. On July 24, just after 6:00 p.m., a bolt on the wooden coaster came loose, causing four cars to crash through a rotten **guardrail**. Twenty-three riders plunged 30 feet (9 m) to the ground. The cars landed on top of them, killing four and injuring seventeen others.

The terrible accident marked the beginning of the end for Krug Park. Soon after the crash, government leaders in Omaha banned amusement parks in the city from running roller coasters. As a result, Krug Park lost business each year until it closed in 1940, and it stood eerily empty for the next 15 years.

The Big Dipper after the accident

In 1955, Krug Park was turned into a city park with baseball fields, a playground, and a swimming pool. The once-abandoned amusement park also got a new name: Gallagher Park.

Scorched Dreams

Pacific Ocean Park, Santa Monica, California

In 1957, amusement park designers spent $10 million creating a seaside wonderland in Santa Monica, California. When Pacific Ocean Park (POP) opened in 1958, its owners hoped it would be as popular as nearby Disneyland. Less than twenty years later, however, the **pier** was far from magical. It was a pile of smoking **rubble**.

The Sea Serpent roller coaster at Pacific Ocean Park

The Ocean Skyway gondola

For just ninety cents, visitors to the newly opened POP could enjoy many different attractions. They included King Neptune's Courtyard, the Sea Circus, and the Westinghouse Enchanted Forest exhibit. The 28-acre (11.3 hectares) park on the pier also featured the Sea Serpent roller coaster and the Ocean Skyway, a **gondola** that took people on a half-mile (.8 km) trip out to sea.

Even with great rides, however, POP had trouble attracting customers. The pier was in a bad part of town, so families didn't feel safe going to the park. By 1965, POP had started to look run-down and was getting fewer and fewer visitors. In October 1967 it closed for good.

Soon after, someone began setting fires on the pier. The first was in December 1969. Six months later an even larger fire broke out at midnight. Thousands watched as the pier's ballroom went up in flames. More fires over the next several years slowly destroyed a park that once had more than 1,000,000 visitors a year. After a final blaze in 1974, the **pilings** that had once held up the pier were all that remained of POP.

The pier after one of the fires

In the 1970s, a group of daredevil teenagers from Santa Monica, nicknamed the Z-Boys, surfed among the ruins of POP. They later became famous for both surfing and skateboarding.

9

Nuclear Ghost Town

Pripyat Amusement Park, Pripyat, Ukraine

The new amusement park in Pripyat was supposed to open on May 1, 1986. To the surprise of the people in town, however, the park opened early on April 27. For a few hours, visitors enjoyed the Ferris wheel, the bumper cars, and other rides. Yet the next day the park was closed, never to open again.

Pripyat after it was abandoned

Why did a brand-new amusement park have such a short history? Less than two miles (3.2 km) away from Pripyat was the Chernobyl **nuclear** power plant. An explosion at the plant on April 26, 1986, destroyed one of its **reactors**, sending clouds of poisonous smoke into the air.

Most of the people who lived in Pripyat worked at Chernobyl. At first, no one was sure how dangerous the situation was. The government didn't want anyone to panic, so those in charge opened the amusement park ahead of schedule to keep people calm. The scope of the danger, however, soon became clear. The amount of **radiation** in the air could kill a person. Several people living in Pripyat became sick right away. The town was **evacuated**, though the people were told they could expect to be back in a few days.

Years later, the town of Pripyat and its amusement park remain empty. The radiation levels are still too dangerous for humans to live there. Wolves and deer now roam the once-bustling city—and the Ferris wheel still sits, waiting for riders to climb aboard.

Today, visitors can take a tour of Pripyat. They go there to see a town frozen in time, filled with the toys, books, and other belongings that people left behind.

An abandoned classroom in Pripyat

One More Ride?

Lake Shawnee Amusement Park, Mercer County, West Virginia

In 1926, C. T. Snidow opened an amusement park in the rolling hills of West Virginia. For 40 years, people enjoyed the carnival rides and swimming pool. When Lake Shawnee closed in 1966, the rides were deserted. Some of the park's visitors, however, refused to go home.

Lake Shawnee Amusement Park after it was closed

Around six people are said to have died during Lake Shawnee's history—and a few are said to still haunt the park. One of the most famous ghost stories dates back to the early 1950s, when a young girl was riding on a twirling swing ride. A truck delivering soda accidentally backed into the swing's path and killed the girl instantly. Since then, the current owner of Lake Shawnee, Gaylord White, claims to have seen her ghost.

The spooky girl has been spotted by another family member as well. Once, when White's father was clearing brush with his tractor, he felt someone leaning on his shoulder. The girl's ghost appeared. She said she wanted his tractor, so he got off and gave it to her. The tractor is still sitting in the field where he stopped working.

On quiet summer nights, other spirits make themselves known. It is rumored that the ghostly voices of children can be heard coming from the abandoned park. Maybe they are waiting for the rides to start again.

The Ferris wheel, now overgrown with weeds, also has a ghostly passenger. A man who some say fell to his death on the ride has been spotted in one of the cars.

Off the Rails

Old Indiana Fun Park, Thorntown, Indiana

There were tons of thrills at Old Indiana Fun Park. Visitors could get soaked on the Waterfall log flume. They could also fly down the hills of the Wildcat roller coaster. The miniature train, however, probably didn't seem very exciting. The train chugged through the woods at a calm 12 miles per hour (19 kph), a tame ride for little kids—or so most people thought.

The train ride at Old Indiana Fun Park

On August 11, 1996, four-year-old Emily Hunt and her family boarded the miniature train ride at Old Indiana Fun Park. They didn't know that the train had derailed 79 times in the past two months. They also were unaware that the **safety inspector** who said the ride worked wasn't **licensed** to inspect rides. The train frequently went too fast because the speedometer was broken and the train's brakes barely worked—if they worked at all.

As the train approached a curve, two cars leaped off the tracks and flipped over. Emily Hunt broke her neck and was **paralyzed** for life. Nancy Jones, Emily's grandmother, was thrown from the train. She died when she slammed into a tree. Emily's grandfather broke his leg, her sister broke an arm, and four others in her family were also injured.

The park's owners claimed they didn't know the ride was dangerous. Yet the park closed later in the year, never to open again. Some of the rides were sold. The rest sit rusting in the Indiana sun, a reminder of one girl's horrible pain.

Abandoned rides at the park

Emily Hunt's family created a charity for people with **spinal cord** injuries. To help raise money, they have hosted annual walkathons.

Blaze and Burn

Electric Park, Kansas City, Missouri

When Electric Park opened, its buildings and towers blazed with the brightness of 100,000 lights. When it closed less than twenty years later, it was still ablaze—only this time it was lit up with yellow and orange flames!

Electric Park lit up at night

On May 19, 1907, a crowd of 53,000 people arrived for the opening of Electric Park. They were excited to take turns on the roller coaster, the giant swing, the Ferris wheel, and the carousel. Beyond the rides, visitors could also enjoy Electric Park's ballroom, ice cream parlor, shooting gallery, alligator farm, and bowling alley. In the evening, a train traveled around the park while colorful fireworks exploded high above the park's lake.

In 1911, a young Walt Disney, who lived only about 15 blocks away, was one of the park's many visitors. Years later, in 1955, he took inspiration from his visits when he built his own amusement park, Disneyland, in California. Like Electric Park, Disneyland had a train that circled the park, and at the end of the day fireworks lit up the night sky.

Unfortunately, Electric Park did not last long. It caught fire in 1925, and most of the park was reduced to ashes. Some claim it was **arson**. Unable to rebuild, the owners closed the park with a final fireworks display.

The famous news reporter Walter Cronkite was just a boy when he saw the fire at Electric Park. Years later, he remembered the event: "Our hill overlooked, a half-dozen blocks away, Electric Park. One night after closing it burned in a spectacular fire. The Ferris wheel seemed to turn as the flames climbed up its sides."

Electric Park

From Good Times to Ghost Town

Six Flags New Orleans, New Orleans, Louisiana

When **Hurricane** Katrina hit Louisiana on August 29, 2005, it hit hard. Thousands of homes were destroyed. More than 1,000 people died. Nearly eighty percent of New Orleans was flooded when the **levees** failed. Some places were damaged so badly that they never recovered—including the local amusement park.

Six Flags after it was flooded

On August 21, 2005, Six Flags was packed with people. They screamed as they swung through the loops of the Jester coaster. They cooled off in the splashes of the giant log flume. They stood in lines that seemed to last forever for the Batman ride. No one knew this day would be the end of the line for the park.

Eight days later, Katrina hit Six Flags. The hurricane caused water from nearby Lake Pontchartrain (PON-chuhr-*trayn*) to flood the park. The entire area was soon covered with water, in some places as high as seven feet (2 m). The water had no place to go, so it sat there for an entire month. By the time it was drained, all of the rides were ruined. There was no way to fix them, so they were left standing.

As the years passed, the surrounding swamps took over the park. Alligators, snakes, and opossums now make the rotted buildings and rusted rides their home. There is talk about turning the area into a mall. Yet today the abandoned park still stands as a reminder of the hurricane's tremendous power.

In 2012, a film crew took over Six Flags. The abandoned amusement park was the perfect spooky setting to film *Percy Jackson: Sea of Monsters*, based on the book by Rick Riordan.

The abandoned park

Eerie Erie Beach

Erie Beach Amusement Park, Ontario, Canada

In 1885, Snake Hill Grove was a simple picnic area. By 1928, it had become a million-dollar amusement park known as Erie Beach. Each day, jam-packed **ferries** and trains full of tourists brought crowds to the park. With all these visitors, how could Erie Beach close for good only two short years later?

Erie Beach Amusement Park

In the 1920s, a day at Erie Beach Amusement Park was an adventure. People could ride a camel in the morning, take a dip in a huge swimming pool after lunch, and dance under the stars to the music of bands that performed at night. In between, visitors could make their hearts race on the Wildcat roller coaster, the Old Mill Chute, and the Flying Ponies carousel.

Unfortunately, after the **Stock Market Crash** in 1929, people were broke. Without money to spend, tourists stopped coming. The park quickly became too expensive to run. The owners closed Erie Beach in 1930, and it has stood abandoned for more than 80 years.

During that time, people came to view the remains of the once-fabulous park. It turned out, however, that there was more to see than old stairs leading nowhere and a crumbling boardwalk. Some visitors claimed to see ghosts. Near the area where the Old Mill Chute once stood, people have spotted a small boy. His ghost lingers where he was said to have fallen out of the ride's boat and drowned decades ago.

Erie Beach Amusement Park is located near Fort Erie, a military base in Canada that is hundreds of years old. During the War of 1812, U.S. troops surprised the Canadians in a deadly battle there. Since that time, some have claimed to see the ghosts of long-dead soldiers wandering around the fort.

The swimming pool at Erie Beach

Accident Park

Action Park, Vernon Township, New Jersey

When Action Park opened in 1978, it was one of the first parks to have water rides. Some of the attractions were so new that they had never been tested before. Unfortunately, many visitors were injured—and some were even killed—as a result. In fact, so many visitors were harmed over the years that some people gave Action Park the nickname Accident Park.

Action Park

One of the most dangerous attractions at Action Park was the Tidal Wave Pool. For 20 minutes at a time, waves as high as 3.3 feet (1 m) slapped at the 500 to 1,000 people in the pool. Those who weren't strong swimmers would sometimes find themselves fighting tall waves in deep water. The 12 lifeguards on duty often rescued as many as 30 people during a weekend. Yet they couldn't save everyone—three people drowned between 1982 and 1987.

Other water rides were almost as scary. The Kayak Experience closed in 1982 after a man was **electrocuted** by an exposed wire. On another ride, the Looping Water Slide, so many people were hurt that it had to be closed after only a month.

In 1996, few were surprised when the park closed for good. The real question was, how had it been allowed to stay open so long?

The Tidal Wave Pool

Not all of the deadly accidents at Action Park involved water. The Alpine Slide was a sled that moved down a concrete track on the side of a mountain. In 1980, a man's sled jumped the tracks. He hit his head on a rock and died.

23

The Comet of Death

Lincoln Amusement Park, Dartmouth, Massachusetts

The jewel of Lincoln Amusement Park was the Comet. For decades, this 3,000-foot-long (914 m) wooden roller coaster was the reason many people came there. Yet in the park's final years, the old coaster was the reason some stayed away.

The Comet

In the 1940s, people who were brave enough to board a car on the Comet quickly climbed up 65 feet (20 m) before the ride went downhill and hit a top speed of 55 miles per hour (86 kph). After two minutes and ten seconds of hills and thrills, the ride was over. Many passengers were scared while riding the wooden roller coaster, but not as frightened as they would come to feel in the years ahead.

One of the ride's scariest accidents took place in 1968 when the Comet's last car detached from the rest of the train, rolled backwards, and **derailed**. The six passengers inside were tossed ten feet (3 m) to the ground. In September 1987, faulty brakes caused the last car to once again derail. It hung off the track while its terrified passengers were trapped inside. Following the disaster, many customers stayed away from the dangerous park. It was forced to close less than three months later.

The abandoned Comet before it was torn down

The Comet still stood with the last car hanging from its tracks after the park was closed. Over the years, people sneaked into the park and set parts of it on fire. What was left of the Comet was finally torn down in 2012.

A Giant Mistake

Gulliver's Kingdom, Kamikuishiki, Japan

The people who created Gulliver's Kingdom started out with a good idea. Why not build an amusement park near Mount Fuji? The **dormant** volcano attracts nearly 25 million tourists a year, so there should be plenty of customers nearby. In addition, why not base the park on the famous book *Gulliver's Travels*? The classic tale features a man who roams the world, and whose travels include a visit to Japan. Yet somehow the park planning took a turn for the weird.

Gulliver's Kingdom

In 1997, Gulliver's Kingdom was built near Mount Fuji. The highlight of the park was based on a famous scene from *Gulliver's Travels*. When Lemuel Gulliver falls asleep in the make-believe land of Lilliput, he awakes to find himself tied to the ground. His captors are a group of six-inch-tall (15 cm) people, called Lilliputians. To recreate this scene, the park built a 147.5-foot-long (45 m) Gulliver lying in the middle of the park. However, the statue didn't do anything. Visitors couldn't climb on it or take a ride around it. Basically, it just lay there.

After visitors looked at the statue, what could they do next? There were no Ferris wheels or roller coasters. Apart from a short train ride and a small town square, the only interesting attractions were a bobsled and **luge** track. Not surprisingly, the park closed after four years. The abandoned attractions stood rotting for another six years. During that time, Gulliver was slowly covered in graffiti until he was demolished in 2007.

The ruins of Gulliver's Kingdom

In addition to the strange statue and few rides, the park was set in a terrible location. It was built next to Aokigahara, also known as Japan's Haunted Forest of Death. According to legend, long ago, during times of **famine**, families would abandon their sick or old in the woods to die. Many claim that the woods are now filled with ghosts.

27

Abandoned Amusement Parks

Erie Beach Amusement Park
Ontario, Canada

The site of a former fort is now home to a ghostly boy.

Old Indiana Fun Park
Thorntown, Indiana

A runaway train causes pain and death for some riders.

Krug Park
Omaha, Nebraska

One of the worst roller-coaster accidents in history takes place.

Lincoln Amusement Park
Dartmouth, Massachusetts

A roller coaster's last ride ends with one of its cars hanging off the track.

NORTH AMERICA

Pacific Ocean Park
Santa Monica, California

A park on a pier burns down.

Action Park
Vernon Township, New Jersey

A park is so dangerous that it becomes known as Accident Park.

Pacific Ocean

Electric Park
Kansas City, Missouri

The park that inspired Walt Disney goes up in flames.

Lake Shawnee Amusement Park
Mercer County, West Virginia

The ghost of a glrl haunts the park where she died.

Six Flags New Orleans
New Orleans, Louisiana

A hurricane turns a Six Flags amusement park into a swamp.

SOUTH AMERICA

Atlantic Ocean

Around the World

Arctic
Ocean

EUROPE

ASIA

AFRICA

Pripyat Amusement Park
Pripyat, Ukraine

A nuclear disaster closes a
park for good.

Gulliver's Kingdom
Kamikuishiki, Japan

A giant tied to the ground is
not a very amusing attraction.

Indian
Ocean

AUSTRALIA

Southern
Ocean

ANTARCTICA

Glossary

abandoned (uh-BAN-duhnd) left empty and no longer being used

arson (AR-suhn) the crime of purposely setting a fire

derailed (dee-RAYLD) ran off the tracks

dormant (DOR-muhnt) when a volcano has not erupted for a very long time, but could erupt again

electrocuted (i-LEK-truh-*kyoot*-id) killed by a strong electric shock

evacuated (i-VAK-yoo-*ayt*-id) when people are moved away from an area because it is dangerous

famine (FAM-in) a shortage of food

ferries (FEHR-eez) boats that travel back and forth between one place and another

gondola (GON-duh-luh) a car that travels along a cable high above the ground

guardrail (GARD-rail) a rail that is used for protection, such as one along the side of a highway or roller coaster track

hurricane (HUR-uh-*kayn*) a storm that forms over the ocean, with heavy rains and fast winds of at least 74 miles per hour (119 kph)

levees (LEV-eez) high walls of dirt and rocks built alongside a river to stop flooding

licensed (LYE-suhnsd) given legal permission to do something

luge (LOOZH) a small sled that a person rides while lying on his or her back

nuclear (NOO-klee-ur) having to do with a type of energy that is produced by splitting atoms

paralyzed (PA-ruh-lyezd) unable to move parts of one's body

penny arcade (PEN-ee ar-KAYD) a building with rows of coin-operated games

pier (PEER) a structure built over water that is used as a walkway or a landing place for boats

pilings (PYE-lingz) long columns driven into the ground that are used to hold up a pier

radiation (*ray*-dee-AY-shuhn) a form of energy that can be very dangerous when not properly controlled

reactors (ree-AK-turz) machines in which a substance called uranium is split to produce nuclear energy

rubble (RUHB-uhl) broken pieces of rock, brick, concrete, and other building materials

safety inspector (SAYF-tee in-SPEK-tur) someone who checks or examines things to make sure they work properly and will not harm anyone

spinal cord (SPY-nuhl KORD) nerve tissue that runs down a person's back and carries messages from the brain to nerves in the body

Stock Market Crash (STOK MAR-kit KRASH) a time in late October 1929 when stocks and bonds suddenly lost value, causing many people to lose their savings

Bibliography

Rabinovitz, Lauren. *Electric Dreamland: Amusement Parks, Movies, and American Modernism.* New York: Columbia University Press (2012).

Rule, Leslie. *Coast to Coast Ghosts: True Stories of Hauntings Across America.* Kansas City, MO: Andrews McMeel (2001).

Read More

Goldish, Meish. *Amazing Amusement Park Rides (So Big Compared to What?).* New York: Bearport (2012).

Goldish, Meish. *Heart-Stopping Roller Coasters (World's Biggest).* New York: Bearport (2010).

Greathouse, Lisa. *How Amusement Parks Work.* Huntington Beach, CA: Teacher Created Materials (2009).

Learn More Online

To learn more about abandoned amusement parks, visit
www.bearportpublishing.com/ScaryPlaces

Index

About the Author

Dinah Williams is an editor and children's book author. Her books include *Shocking Seafood; Slithery, Slimy, Scaly Treats; Monstrous Morgues of the Past; Haunted Houses;* and *Spooky Cemeteries,* which won the Children's Choice Award. She lives in Cranford, New Jersey.